Arnold Friberg's Little Christmas Book

THE HOLY FAMILY

Arnold Friberg's Little Christmas Book

The Bethlehem Press, 5867 Tolcate Lane, Salt Lake City, Utah

Thanks and deep appreciation are here expressed to friends for the use in this book of the following pictures: for the three scenes from "The Ten Commandments," Paramount Pictures Corporation, for the farmer and boy, Utah-Idaho Sugar Company; for Ballantyne and his Sunday School, the Deseret Sunday School Union; for the three Mounted Police subjects, The Northwest Paper Company; for "The Music of Christmas from Temple Square," Station KSL-TV; for the carol singers by the church, Beneficial Life Insurance Company and The Improvement Era magazine. All these pictures are used by permission.

FIRST EDITION
November, 1959

To Hedve, my wife, whom the Lord gave me

HOW AND WHY THIS
LITTLE CHRISTMAS BOOK WAS BORN

"My soul delighteth in plainness." So spoke Nephi twenty-five hundred years ago. Prophet though he was, and privileged, as were Moses and Abraham, to see ahead through the future centuries of time, yet he would scarcely have foreseen a struggling twentieth century illustrator whose painting style would be rooted in Nephi's own prophetic words.

Yet if someone were to ask me for a statement of artistic creed, I could do no better than to quote the above words of Nephi. For whether in speech or in paint, I have never understood anything but plain talk. In painting a horse, for instance, my sole aim is to make him look like a horse looks, and when the picture is done, I'd rather have it please a ranch hand than an art critic. So in painting a scriptural subject, it is not so important to please the museum or the art expert as it is to bring the story to life for those who love the word of God.

Since I was a boy, I haved loved each year to read or hear the wonderful Christmas story. And even as a boy, the words of the Holy Bible were always stronger and richer than anyone's retold version. They just couldn't compete with Luke and Matthew!

But speakers on Christmas programs began to avoid the Bible story ("because you've all heard about the shepherds and the wise men so many times") in favor of a pioneer Christmas tale, the first Christmas in America, a sermon on the meaning of Christmas, or perhaps even a medieval legend or a fairy tale. I can't count the years since I heard the Bible story read, verbatim, right out the Book, in church at Christmastime. And I miss it.

A similar avoidance was apparent in the commercially available Christmas cards. They were lovely, but they seemed to miss something.

But perhaps this was due to a personal feeling about the Bible story which it would be unfair to expect another artist to capture.

In any event, since at Christmas we wanted to get back to the very roots of the Holy Season, I had no choice but to produce our own cards.

Being by trade an artist, or, as the critics say, a mere illustrator, I took my brush in hand and told the story as simply and as plainly as I could, and lettered in the scriptural text alongside.

To our complete but pleasant surprise, these cards were so well received that it soon became obvious that many people of all faiths were apparently as hungry for the simple Bible story as we were.

Since so many kind friends expressed their enjoyment of the pictures, we felt that many more could enjoy them if they were made available in a printed collection. The result is this little Christmas book.

It might be called some sort of a Christmas scrap book, for the pictures and hand lettering included in it have been produced over the years for a number of purposes other than for our Christmas cards, and they have been gathered together here for the first time. Some were done for magazine covers and illustrations, some for advertisements, calendars, art prints, motion picture work, and a few just for their own sweet sake alone.

Not all of them are Biblical, but I trust the reader will find them sufficiently in tune with the Christmas spirit to warrant their being included in this book.

Some critics have said that one artist cannot do rugged outdoor and western subjects and then "turn around" and do religious art.

But actually these two fields are closely related. For if in a western subject with men and animals all taking their right and proper places in the wondrous world of Nature, the artist can tell of the glory of the Creator's handiwork; and if in a religious subject he can tell of real people, sons and daughters of the living God, stumbling and falling and triumphing in a real world; then the two subjects fuse into one and there is really no difference at all. For all matter is finally spiritual.

This little book is not intended to be an exhaustive reference work. For the intensive scholar there are already any number of such excellent texts. Here only such mention is made of historical details as will be of help in binding together the old and the new, and I trust will add just a bit to the reader's overall understanding and appreciation of the timeless grandeur of God's eternal plan.

A. Friberg

JT IS GOOD to be a child sometimes, and never better than at Christmas, when its mighty founder was a child Himself.

Charles Dickens

O little town of Bethlehem

How still we see thee lie.

Above thy deep and dreamless sleep

The silent stars go by.

Yet in thy dark street shineth

The everlasting Light.

The hopes and fears of all the years

Are met in thee tonight.

How silently, how silently
    The wondrous gift is giv'n.
So God imparts to human hearts
    The blessings of His heav'n.
No ear may hear His coming
    Yet in this world of sin
Where meek souls will receive Him still
    The dear CHRIST enters in.

A DeCree from

CÆSAR AVGVSTVS

AND IT CAME TO PASS IN
THOSE DAYS THAT THERE WENT OVT A DECREE
FROM CÆSAR AVGVSTVS THAT ALL THE WORLD
SHOVLD BE TAXED. AND ALL WENT TO
BE TAXED, EVERY ONE INTO HIS OWN CITY.
AND JOSEPH ALSO WENT VP FROM GALILEE, OVT
OF THE CITY OF NAZARETH, INTO JVDÆA, VNTO
THE CITY OF DAVID, WHICH WAS CALLED BETHLEHEM,
(Because he was of the House and lineage
of David), TO BE TAXED WITH MARY, HIS
ESPOVSED WIFE,

From the Gospel according to Luke

THE POWER . . . AND THE GLORY

OME! ! If ever one power has dominated an era of history, it was Imperial Rome; and at the time when Jesus was born, she was at the very zenith of her dazzling strength.

Order was everywhere. Rome ruled the land and the sea. Her cities were clean. Her highways were stoutly built, numerous, and above all safe for the traveller, for Rome tolerated no thievery. Her laws were stern but just. The tramp of her marching legions struck respect, even terror, into the hearts of those who might have opposed her. And her taxes were almost unbearably heavy.

At the very pinnacle of this vast and organized might sat the Emperor Octavian, so known for his august and sober responsibility that his very name was called Caesar Augustus. Not yet had the Imperial throne yielded to mad and degenerate tyrants.

Of all lands in the empire, Judaea and Galilee were nearly the farthest distant from Rome. But whether near or far, everyone must go to his own city to be taxed. For there must be order in the empire.

Rome was Pagan, yet tolerant of other faiths—not out of piety or of respect for others, but out of mere indifference. What was one more god, or a few more gods, to citizens who already worshipped so many?

Rome was powerful, but her power was mortal, and of this world only. And just as mortality is foreign to eternity, so the power of this earth is stranger to the real glory of Eternal Life.

The Legionairre here pictured stands lonely guard, but secure in the power of Rome. Little does he know, or even suspect, the infinite glory passing, now, within his very sight. It is too humble for him to recognize, too quiet, too lacking in pomp and pretense.

Earthly empires come and go. The power of Rome has crumbled. But the tender glory of the babe of Bethelehem has never dimmed.

HOW THE SHEPHERDS HEARD
THE WONDERFUL CHRISTMAS STORY

And there were in the same country shepherds abiding in the field, keeping watch over their flock by night. And, lo, the Angel of the LORD came upon them, and the glory of the LORD shone round about them: and they were sore afraid.

And the Angel said unto them, Fear not: for, behold, I bring you good tidings of great joy, which shall be to all people.

For unto you is born this day in the city of David a SAVIOUR, which is CHRIST the LORD.

AND suddenly there was with the Angel a multitude of the Heavenly host praising **God**, and saying, Glory to **God** in the highest, and on Earth peace, good will toward men.

From the Gospel according to Luke

THE SHEPHERDS IN THE FIELDS

THE NATIVITY

"The shepherds they, to Bethlehem did they g

o see whe'er it were so or no, To see if Christ were born or no, To set men free"

S uch people as the Biblical shepherds, who were privileged to witness rare and glorious historical events, are bound to arouse our interest in the question of who they might have been.

Were they merely average shepherds tending their flocks for a living? Or were they Levite priests, assigned to guard the many sheep being especially raised, without blemish, for use in sacrifice in the Temple at Jerusalem? If they were Levites, how right it is that the Heavenly Host should have appeared to them, for does not the Levitical, or Aaronic Priesthood hold the keys to the ministering of angels?

Perhaps, as they kept watch over their flocks that night, they might have earnestly discussed what had happened to their fellow-Levite Zacharias, who only a few months before had seen an angel in the Holy Place of the Temple and had learned that he was to be the father of John, the Baptist, and had been struck dumb until the child was born.

The night was broken into four "watches" of three hours apiece. So that the shepherds on duty may perhaps have heard the "glad tidings of great joy" while their companions slept.

The reproduction on the opposite page is a full-sized detail taken from "The Shepherds in the Fields." For those readers who wish to study the brushwork and details of clothing and facial characterization, it is shown here the actual size of the original.

In painting this picture, it has been my dedicated aim to portray real people witnessing a real and sacred historical event, and to catch a momentary glimpse of the awesome grandeur of the wonderful thing that happened there that night, on the plains of Judaea.

THE WISE MEN FROM THE EAST

ow when Jesus was born in Bethlehem of Judæa in the days of Herod the king, behold, there came wise men from the east to Jerusalem,

Saying, Where is He that is born King of the Jews? for we have seen His star in the east, and are come to worship Him.

When Herod the king had heard these things, he was troubled, and all Jerusalem with him.

And when he had gathered all the chief priests and scribes of the people together, he demanded of them where CHRIST should be born.

And they said unto him, In Bethlehem of Judæa: for thus it is written by the prophet,

And thou Bethlehem, in the land of Juda, art not the least among the princes of Juda: for out of thee shall come a Governor, that shall rule my people ISRAEL."

THEN Herod, when he had privily called the wise men, enquired of them diligently what time the star appeared.

And he sent them to Bethlehem, and said, Go and search diligently for the young child; and when ye have found him, bring me word again, that I may come and worship him also.

When they had heard the king, they departed; and, lo, the star, which they saw in the east, went before them, till it came and stood over where the young child was.

When they saw the star, they rejoiced with exceeding great joy.

And when they were come into the house, they saw the young child with Mary his mother, and fell down, and worshipped Him: and when they had opened their treasures, they presented unto Him gifts; gold, and frankincense, and myrrh.

And being warned of God in a dream that they should not return to Herod, they departed into their own country another way.

FOLLOWING THE STAR

So many legends have been spun about the Wise Men that it is refreshing to return and drink of the cool and simple Scriptural truth, and to separate fact from legend.

While in this painting I have pictured the customary "three wise men," it is noteworthy that the Bible makes no mention of their number.

Legend has given them names — Balthazar the Greek, Melchior the Egyptian, and Gaspar the Ethiopian. But a glance at a map will show that all of these countries lie to the west of the Holy Land, whereas the Bible points out that the wise men came from the east. So that

they might have come from such lands as Syria, Babylonia, perhaps even from as far away as India.

But since Matthew didn't consider their names or their number of enough importance to record, it would seem well to consider their purpose rather than their names, or where they came from.

For regardless of the world's learning, it is still the truest wisdom to follow the Star of Bethlehem. And wise men will still come to Jerusalem, saying, Where is He that is born King of the Jews? for we have seen his star in the east, and are come to worship Him.

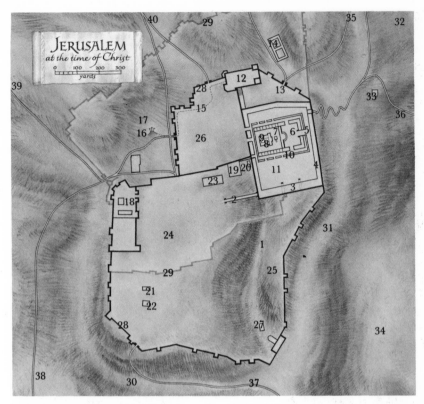

JERUSALEM
at the time of Christ
0 100 200 300
yards

1 Tyropoean Valley   2 Bridge leading to the temple   3 Royal porch   4 Solomon's porch
5 Corinthian (Beautiful) gate   6 Court of women   7 Altar of sacrifice   8 Holy place
9 Holy of holies   10 Wall separating Jews from Gentiles   11 Court of Gentiles   12 Fortress
of Antonia   13 Sheep gate   14 Pool of Bethesda   15 Way of the Cross   16 Golgotha
17 Garden tomb   18 Palace of Herod   19 Market place   20 Sanhedrin   21 House of Cai-
aphas   22 House of the Last Supper   23 Palace of the Hasmonaeans   24 Upper city
25 Lower city   26 Suburb   27 Pool of Siloam   28 Wall at the time of Christ   29 Later
wall   30 Valley of Hinnom   31 Valley of the Kidron   32 Mount of Olives   33 Garden of
Gethsemane   34 Mount of Offence   35 Road to Jericho   36 Road to Bethany   37 Road
to the Dead Sea   38 Road to Bethlehem, Gaza   39 Road to Joppa   40 Road to Caesarea

Jerusalem the Golden! The City of the Great King! The Holy
City! Israel's poets could hardly find words of praise sufficient
to honor the great metropolis that David had made his capital. She was
not only the largest city in the land that stretched "from Dan to Beer-
sheba," but her immortal greatness rested in the reverent affection with
which she was held fast in all the hearts of Israel. During the dark days

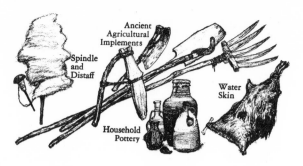

Spindle and Distaff

Ancient Agricultural Implements

Water Skin

Household Pottery

of captivity and exile, Israel sang, "If I forget thee, O Jerusalem, let my right hand forget her cunning."

Josephus, the Jewish historian who lived in Jerusalem at the time of Christ, has left us a remarkable and priceless treasure in his written description of the times and of the city, including even numbers and measurements of columns and stairways in Herod's temple.

Today's visitors to Jerusalem cannot walk on the very streets that Jesus knew, for the accumulated rubble of two thousand years have buried those original streets a good thirty feet below the present city.

And we must be cautious in basing our concept of the ancient city on the dark, narrow streets and questionable conditions of Old Jerusalem as it stands in Moslem hands today. For in the Saviour's time, when Israel lived there, the streets were broad enough to allow a number of vehicles, animals, and people to pass freely, and white stones were used in the paving. There was no garbage or refuse in the streets, for so strict were both Roman and Jewish law in regard to cleanliness and sanitation, that not even a fowl could be kept within the city walls.

The necessity for such improved conditions becomes clearer as we learn to appreciate the vast scale and magnificence of those ancient civilizations and their extremely numerous populations.

Several times yearly, at feast seasons, hundreds of thousands of pilgrims clogged the wide Roman roads, and as they approached the Holy City they sang certain Psalms, that are known in the Bible as the "Psalms of Ascent." At such times it was the duty of those whose privilege it was to live in Jerusalem to open their doors to friend and stranger alike.

With such numbers seeking shelter, it is easy to understand how even in the neighboring town of Bethelehem, there was no room at the inn.

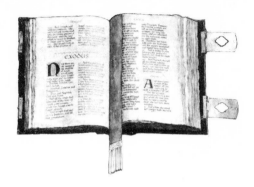

Sometimes we hear of the stern Old Testament "God of wrath" almost as if He were a different God from that of the New Testament. But from the beginning He has always been the same.

When willful men's own conduct has been deserving of punishment, then God has rightly been just and stern. But in the Old Testament as well as the New, He has always loved His children here below, and He has desired nothing more than their joy and their eternal welfare.

"Adam fell, that man might be." Ever since the time of that portentous event, known as "The Fall," when man became subject to illness and suffering and death, a kind and merciful, albeit just God had promised that He would send to the world a Saviour, who should come to the earth and redeem mankind from sin, even from death itself. "For as in Adam all died, so in Christ shall all be made alive."

All through Old Testament times, prophets were raised up to foretell His coming. Laws and ordinances were given that would prepare men's minds for His advent. As the Lamb of God would be pure and unspotted by sin, even so, in similitude, animals offered to the Lord in sacrifice must also be choice and without blemish.

During the lonely days of hardship and exile, Israel was cheered and strengthened by this promise of a Redeemer. And to those who were of the lineage of David, it was especially comforting and glorious to know that through this very line would be born The Great Emmanuel!

THE FIRST PASSOVER

Each year ancient Israel observed a number of feasts, solemn or joyous according to its purpose or the historical event it commemorated. The feast of the Passover, observed in Old Testament times and kept to this day by those who still live the law of Moses, was a solemn one, not only commemerating Israel's Divine deliverance from Egypt, but also foretelling by the symbolic sacrifice of the paschal lamb, the future sacrifice that would one day be made by the Lamb of God.

The scene above, like the following two pictures, is from the many paintings I did for Cecil B. DeMille in the course of producing the motion picture "The Ten Commandments." Mr. DeMille always wanted me to paint a companion picture to this one, of The Last Supper. The two subjects would be an ideal pair. For it must be remembered that the Last Supper was no ordinary dinner, but was a Passover meal.

It should also be realized that the Lamb eaten at the Last Supper was the last truly paschal lamb; for the law of Moses was now fulfilled, and within a very few hours the true Lamb of God would be sacrificed on Golgotha for the sins of the world.

On the table are the bitter herbs, to remind Israel of the bitterness of captivity. In the background is being baked the unleavened "bread of haste," and the wine is partaken of with psalms of thanksgiving. At the Last Supper, the Saviour altered the purpose of the bread and wine to that of the Sacrament. "This do," He said, "in remembrance of me."

THE FINDING OF MOSES

In this painting, also done for "The Ten Commandments," I have tried to capture some of the same kind of spirit that might go into a Nativity scene, and for a reason that I believe is important.

For how remarkably similar and parallel are many events in the lives of the prophet Moses and the Lord Jesus Christ.

Each was born into the humblest and lowliest of earthly circumstances, and as an infant each had to be shielded and hidden from an oppressive and murderous heathen king who feared the might of Israel. They were in each case protected by Divine power.

Each was to challenge and triumph over the power of earthly rulers.

Each was to climb a mountain alone, there to spend forty days and forty nights in lonely solitude, in fasting and in prayer, and in close communion with his Heavenly Father.

Each spent his early boyhood in Egypt and his closing moments of mortal life on a mountaintop.

Each in his time gave to the world new laws and concepts that ever since have been the supreme guide for all nations, kindreds, and tongues.

God Himself compared Moses to the Messiah who was to come when He said: "Blessed art thou, Moses, for I, the Almighty, have chosen thee, and thou shalt be made stronger than many waters; for they shall obey thy command as if thou wert God. And I have a work for thee, Moses, my son; and thou art in the similitude of mine Only Begotten; and mine Only Begotten is and shall be the Saviour, for he is full of grace and truth."

When Moses was gone it was written, "And there arose not a prophet since in Israel like unto Moses whom the Lord knew face to face."

The Ten Commandments are a part of what is called the law of Moses. Yet it was not Moses himself who actually gave the law. Like all prophets, he was but a true and faithful servant, the earthly and human instrument through which Jehovah gave His law to mankind.

The law of Moses remained in force for nearly 1300 years. It is important to realize that Jesus never broke that law, although He constantly taught that "the letter killeth but the spirit giveth life."

"And He said unto them: Marvel not that I said unto you that old things had passed away, and that all things become new. Behold, I say unto you that the law is fulfilled that was given unto Moses.

"Behold, I am he that gave the law, and I am he who covenanted with my people Israel; therefore, the law in me is fulfilled, for I have come to fulfill the law; therefore it hath an end.

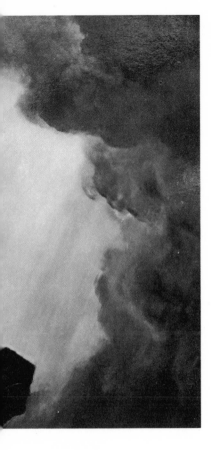

THE GIVING OF THE LAW

"Behold, I do not destroy the prophets, for as many as have not been fulfilled in me, verily I say unto you, shall all be fulfilled.

"And because I said unto you that old things have passed away, I do not destroy that which hath been spoken concerning things which are to come.

"For behold, the covenant which I have made with my people is not all fulfilled; but the law which was given unto Moses hath an end in me.

"Behold, I am the law, and the light. Look unto me, and endure to the end, and ye shall live; for unto him that endureth to the end will I give eternal life. Behold, I have given unto you the commandments; therefore keep my commandments. And this is the law and the prophets, for they truly testified of me."   *from 3. Nephi, 15:3*

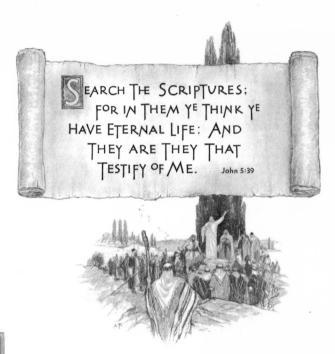

SEARCH THE SCRIPTURES;
FOR IN THEM YE THINK YE
HAVE ETERNAL LIFE: AND
THEY ARE THEY THAT
TESTIFY OF ME.   John 5:39

Scriptural truths have always illumined human paths and labors. The Bible excerpt quoted in the picture on the opposite page was one of Mr. DeMille's favorite passages, for it ties together the Old Testament with the New. He hung this painting as a sort of centerpiece of his office wall, so that he could see it as he worked. "Sinai," he often said, "sheds the same light as the Star of Bethlehem."

In this painting, Moses is shown in his true and proper relationship to the Saviour. Bathed and strengthened and ennobled in the wondrous Light of Christ, he has become a great and a mighty prophet himself; yet he is in no way co-equal with the Son of God.

No one knew this better than Moses himself. He was the humblest servant in the vineyard. His life is an example of magnificent selflessness.

It might be asked, since this is a Christmas picture, why did I paint into it the crosses on Calvary? Christmas commemorates the birth, not the death of Christ. But His birth is meaningful only because of His life. When He lay swaddled in a manger, the angels sang in the sky; for they knew that in the great redeeming plan of God, He would one day walk the lone and bitter road to Golgotha, there to die and there to rise again, conquering death in glorious and triumphant Resurrection!

FOR HAD YE BELIEVED MOSES YE WOULD HAVE BELIEVED ME

John 5:46

THE LIGHT AND THE LAW

A PECULIAR TREASURE

As we look at the Holy Land and consider what a small spot it is, all the more remarkable becomes the immense influence that this tiny plot of ground has had upon the nations of the earth.

Here lay the crossroads of ancient trade, both by sea and by the great land caravan routes. Here, each under its own standard, lived the tribes of Israel, who were to form the two great nations of Ephraim, or Israel, and Judah. Here David watered his flocks and struck his psalmist's harp. Here prophets and angels proclaimed the burning word of God. Here reigned Solomon in all his glory, and here the conquering hordes of Nebuchadnezzar ravished and burned and laid waste the cities.

Here also lived Jesus of Nazareth.

Over four thousand years ago, the Lord made a solemn promise to Abraham that through his posterity "all the nations of the earth will be blessed." It is because of Abraham that the Holy Land has been, and is today, sacred ground to Christian, Jew, and Mohammedan alike.

Rome and Greece and Babylon each gave to civilization her own gifts of learning and beauty. But in Israel alone burned the tiny light that kept alive God's truth in the world. In a vast sea of heathen idolatry, Israel was the keeper of the flame.

It was from this land and through this people that the Lord gave us the priceless and sacred words of the Holy Scriptures.

And when the time came, it was through Israel that God gave to the world His greatest gift — His only-begotten Son.

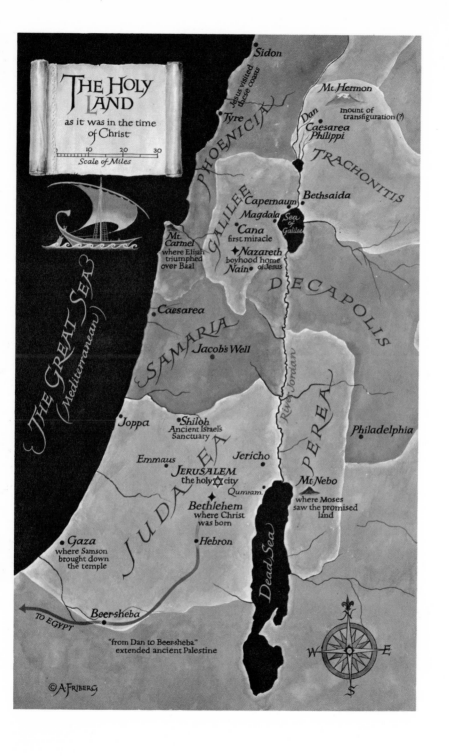

As sang the Psalmist, "The earth is the Lord's, and the fullness thereof." It is not difficult to understand that He who created Heaven and Earth shall also command any part of it. Who causes the winds to blow can also still them. Learned men have so often failed to

E STILL"

fathom His power that it is no wonder that He spoke of "the peace that passeth understanding." And as once Jesus calmed the deadly gale on the Sea of Galilee, so today, if we will seek Him, He will speak, and say, "Peace, be still," and His healing spirit will still the storms of life.

THE SOWER AND THE REAPER

How often in the Lord's wisdom He has taught man through the humble familiar things he understands the best. When Jesus walked the earth, He spoke of the times and the seasons, of seed time and harvest, of the soil, of the wheat and the chaff, and of the faith of the tiny mustard seed.

Since the earth began, the scriptural instructions of the Lord to man have been timeless, eternal, and infinitely rich in wisdom.

Consider, for example, the 28th verse of the very first book in the Bible — Genesis. Much too often we hear quoted only the first portion of this directive that the Lord gave to Adam — "Multiply and replenish the earth." But the whole command is to "Multiply and replenish the earth, and subdue it."

The editors of "The U and I Cultivator" saw in the latter part of this scripture a divine injunction to all those who live close to the soil, and as a result I drew this picture for their cover.

This farmer is passing on to his son the experienced knowledge he will need to "subdue" the earth. But at the same time he is teaching

"...*Replenish the Earth, and subdue it.*" *Genesis 1:28*

him the responsibility to "replenish" the land as well as to draw out its goodness and bounty.

"The earth is the Lord's, and the fullness thereof." The land is not ours to waste. For, in humble thanksgiving, do we not recognize that this is "a land choice above all others"?

So in our day the ancient scripture stands.

RICHARD BALLANTYNE

A MAN AND A DREAM

The American frontier was not an easy place to live. But men of God have always been frontiersmen.

For men of dedicated purpose grow strong under trial, and their determination to conquer difficulties often results in a service that continues to bless mankind long after the pioneer is gone.

Such a man was Richard Ballantyne.

In his native Scotland he had been engaged in Sunday School work, and when he had come to America and trekked West with the Mormon pioneers, he desired to found a Sunday School for the young people there in the Valley of the Great Salt Lake.

"The gospel of Christ," he said, "is so precious to me that I cannot bring myself to withhold it from the children."

Brigham Young heartily approved the plan, and with Scottish grit Ballantyne set his hand to the task. He went to Big Cottonwood Canyon and there quarried blocks of granite, slung them low under an ox-drawn cart, and slowly and heavily brought them down the long twenty-odd miles to be used in his foundation. He dug a pit, and used the earth to mold adobe bricks for his wall. With an axe he felled trees in mountain forests and hauled them to the sawmill, there to be shaped into timbers for his floors, doorways, roof, and other woodwork.

So, while he and his wife and family lived in a wagon closeby, he built with his own hands a house with an especially large living, or meeting room. Pioneer work though it was, his building was a labor of rugged love, warm and stout, and now he had a place in which he could hold the first Sunday School in the Rocky Mountains.

THE PIONEER SUNDAY SCHOOL

On the cold, snowy morning of December 9th, 1849, the door of Richard Ballantyne's new Sunday School opened to receive the first arrivals. Ranging in age from 8 to 14 years, they came trooping in early, for Sunday School was held at 8 A.M. in order that the children could be out in time to go to church again at 10.

There is a bronze plaque now to mark where the building stood at what is now 1st west and 3rd south streets in Salt Lake City. In the living room was a large stone fireplace, and the benches were made of logs split in two, with some rude legs added to hold them firm.

This painting was commissioned as part of the Centennial observances marking the event, and so was done in 1949, just one hundred years after the opening of Richard Ballantyne's frontier Sunday School.

Such historical pictures as this require laborious and fervent research in every detail. We had written descriptions of the building, and fortunately a search located a scratched but excellent tintype of Ballantyne at just the right age. Being in actuality a tall, handsome, rawboned Scot, he required no pictorial idealizing. His figure was posed by Lorin Moench, a descendant who resembles him.

For the other figures, my models were the neighborhood children. Although only those who were actually posing were allowed in my basement studio on Kenwood Street, the windows were nearly always filled with the lively, curious faces of children and dogs. While posing for the dark haired boy in the middle of the first row, all spruced up in authentic costume and flowing bow tie, my model Stephen Stutz was grievously heckled by the window art critics. And when two of the girls were posing, the boys in the window serenaded them with such then-popular songs as "Baby, It's Cold Outside!"

That wonderful stone fireplace I found up in American Fork Canyon, and many of the props came from Horace Sorensen's Pioneer Village Museum, and from the Historical Museum on Temple Square.

The only model I didn't have to costume was the cat.

As I painted, I wondered — "What were the children taught on that first Sunday School morning?" No one knows, but since the date was in December, only two weeks before Christmas, perhaps in their very first lesson they learned the old, old story of the shepherds and the Wise Men, and of the child who was born in Bethlehem so long ago.

A·FRIBERG

THE CHRISTMAS TREE

H aving painted many frontier subjects, one year I did this picture for our Christmas card, accompanied by a hearty Western
Christmas wish. It shows the kind of country you might find in Montana,
up near the Canadian border. The Indian is a Cree or a Blackfoot,
wearing the Hudson's Bay blanket coat so typical of the northern tribes.

The ruggedness of frontier life had its compensations in the warmth
of human companionship, made even richer at Christmastime, and as
pictured here, the joy of bringing in your own Chrtismas tree!

THE CHRISTMAS PACKET   A constable of the North

Mounted Police, with his Indian guide, on their way to bring gifts and mail to an outpost of civilization. With good luck they will make it in time for Christmas.

THE OLD, OLD STORY

God holds us responsible for our own actions. Jesus taught mercy and compassion and love, but He never violated justice.

When men walk in honor and truth, and when their laws are just and fairly administered, then it is that men are acting in a way pleasing before the Lord. For basic law all flows from Divine law.

The pictures of the Northwest Mounted Police shown in this book are a very few from among the many dozens of such subjects I have painted through the years for The Northwest Paper Company.

In doing preparatory study for these pictures, I have come to know a number of these police (now called the Royal Canadian Mounted Police, or the R.C.M.P.) and from all personal contact as well as from research into the history of the force, I have come to appreciate why they have gained the respect of decent people everywhere.

In the rugged and sparsely settled Canadian vastness, these men were not alone the sole government, but were often the only doctor, teacher, counsellor, and link with Christian civilization. They dealt fairly with red man and white man alike, and because of their human consideration and their devotion to real justice, Canada was spared the bloody Indian wars so common on our side of the border.

Their history makes you feel proud of mankind.

If the Mountie on the opposite page resembles the figure of Ballantyne teaching his pioneer Sunday School, it is because anyone who gives time to the teaching and guiding of youth is a Richard Ballantyne. Without hundreds like him, the greatest of leaders would be helpless.

"GOD REST YE, MERRIE GENTLEMEN"

The singing of carols at Christmastime is a happy custom that has cheered mankind in all Christian ages and that has survived wars and all manner of evil and calamity. There is something about these simple, enduringly beautiful songs that speaks directly to the heart and to the spirit, and have continually brought men back to the equally simple, enduringly beautiful story of the Babe of Bethlehem.

Perhaps the best loved of all the carols is "Silent Night, Holy Night," which also came to be called "The Song from Heaven."

Aside from the beauty of the song itself, I have a special personal affection for this carol, for at the close of the bitter European warfare in 1945, our infantry outfit found ourselves in the Austrian town of Oberndorf, and on that first night of peace we visited the very church where in 1818 Franz Gruber and Joseph Mohr had first written "Stille Nacht, Heilige Nacht."

NEW DAYS, NEW WAYS

This is the main title card which I prepared for the C B S Christmas television broadcast of the Salt Lake Tabernacle Choir.

The wonderful thing about the Tabernacle Choir is that you never notice the musical "arrangements." All you feel is the rich, warm, ringing truth of the Christmas spirit. Instead of "Art," you feel the power of conviction. That's rarer. I try to paint the way the choir sings.

As the minstrels of earlier times brought the songs of Christmas to those who could hear, so in our day the same songs are brought to millions of listeners who cherish the Christmas story.

But whatever the time or the place, or the year, or the century, the song still swells in the hearts of men, of praise and of adoration, and of thanksgiving for the pure and redeeming truth of Christmas, foretelling the promised day "when every knee shall bow and every tongue confess that Jesus is the Christ."

"JOY TO THE WORL

"HE LORD IS COME"

"ONE FOLD AND ONE SHEPHERD"

"After this manner pray ye,"

UR FATHER who art
in Heaven, Hallowed
be Thy name. Thy
kingdom come. Thy will be done
on earth, as it is in Heaven.
Give us this day our daily bread,
and forgive us our debts, as we
forgive our debtors.
And let us not be led into
temptation, but deliver us from evil.
For Thine is the kingdom, and
the power and the glory, forever.

Amen

HERE THE Spirit of the Lord is, there is Liberty.

2. Corinthians 3:17